DRONES AND THE GOVERNMENT

JENNIFER CULP

ROSEN
PUBLISHING

New York

Published in 2017 by The Rosen Publishing Group
29 East 21st Street, New York, NY 10010

Library of Congress Cataloging-in-Publication Data

Names: Culp, Jennifer, 1985– author.
Title: Drones and the government / Jennifer Culp.
Description: First edition. | New York : Rosen Publishing, 2017. | Series:
Inside the world of drones | Audience: Grades 7 to 12. | Includes
bibliographical references and index.
Identifiers: LCCN 2016028148 | ISBN 9781508173472 (library bound)
Subjects: LCSH: Drone aircraft—Juvenile literature. | Technological
innovations—Juvenile literature.
Classification: LCC UG1242.D7 C85 2017 | DDC 623.74/69—dc23
LC record available at https://lccn.loc.gov/2016028148

Manufactured in China

CONTENTS

INTRODUCTION

Not long ago, unmanned aerial vehicles (UAVs), more commonly known as drones, may have sounded like something out of science fiction. As small as a toy or as big as an airplane, capable of carrying camera technology that can film an entire 3-mile (4.8-kilometer) geographic area down to 6 inches (15 centimeters) in detail, of delivering medical supplies or firing weapons upon remote command—drones are in fact quite real, and they are currently revolutionizing many aspects of our modern world.

Drones may be used for surveillance, logistics, research, search-and-rescue missions, warfare, and various media including photography and broadcasting. Civilian hobbyists fly small quadcopters that weigh less than 10 pounds (4.5 kilograms). The military uses Predator drones with 60-foot (18.2-meter) wingspans to survey hostile terrain and even fire missiles at enemy targets. Drones examine the interior of erupting volcanoes and chart hard-to-reach terrain. Drones can locate missing persons and deliver medical supplies to remote areas.

Any new technology will be accompanied with growing pains, however. Much consideration must be given to how their use impacts privacy rights and many other concerns. Government agencies responsible for supervising appropriate uses of this new technology and preventing potential criminal use must tread carefully. Citizens and

A UNIVERSITY OF CALIFORNIA, DAVIS, DRONE OPERATOR TESTS A UAV IN ARBUCKLE, CALIFORNIA. THE SCHOOL IS ONE OF FIVE TESTING DRONES FOR CROP DUSTING.

government officials both are at the dawn of a new era of unmanned flight.

In the United States, the Federal Aviation Administration (FAA) oversees airspace. In this early stage of the drone era, the FAA is at the forefront of creating new drone-specific rules. For the time being, the United States employs some of the strictest drone restrictions in the world, essentially forbidding commercial drone use and imposing tight supervision on public drone projects.

At the same time, government agencies, such as United States Customs and Border Protection (CBP), are beginning to utilize drones in domestic airspace and will only expand their use in the future. But the scope and details of government-sanctioned uses are not clear to the average citizen, raising concerns about privacy and government overreach.

In the private sector, companies such as online retailer Amazon chafe against domestic drone restriction, eager to incorporate drone-assisted delivery and other functionality into their existing services. Scientific research organizations bemoan the necessity of receiving slow, tedious FAA approval for each individual project while also recognizing the need for law to protect wildlife and natural resources.

Meanwhile, individual drone hobbyists are allowed to fly after completing a low-cost national registration, but the question of adequate enforcement of existing laws comes into question: How do you catch someone using a drone inappropriately, and when you do, what sort of punishment should the person receive? It will be very interesting to see how drone legislation and usage develop over the course of the next decades as federal, local, and international governments work to safely integrate unmanned aircraft into our daily lives and the economy.

CHAPTER 1

THE DRONE REVOLUTION

D rones, also called unmanned aircraft systems (UASs) or unmanned aerial vehicles (UAVs), were originally developed for military purposes. From the first forays into the air in 1911, military engineers searched for ways to reduce risk to human pilots.

During World War I, the US Navy came up with the idea of "air torpedoes," which were actually just unmanned biplanes catapulted up into the sky to fly on their own. These air torpedoes were not very effective and usually just crashed or flew away, ending up lost at sea. During World War II, the navy decided that unmanned aerial vehicles might stay on course better with some human assistance. Pilots flew explosive-filled B-24 bombers up into the air and then were meant to parachute out to safety

A DRONE SITS ON A FRENCH NAVY VESSEL AT A CELEBRATION OF DIPLOMATIC TIES BETWEEN FRANCE AND VIETNAM. IT WAS IN VIETNAM THAT DRONES WERE FIRST UTILIZED, DURING THE US-LED VIETNAM WAR IN THE LATE 1960S.

while the plane continued on a radio-guided course to destroy its target.

This effort failed even more tragically than the first: future president John F. Kennedy's older brother was killed piloting a bomb-filled plane that exploded prematurely. In the aftermath of these disasters, the rise of improved rocket technology discouraged heavy investment in unmanned aerial weaponry in the mid-twentieth century. The 1960s and 1970s saw US Air Force engineers—and the militaries of foreign nations—turn their attention toward developing unmanned aircraft for surveillance purposes instead of remote killing. Drones with limited abilities were used by the United States during the Vietnam War and also by the Israeli Defense Forces (IDF) during various conflicts with neighboring Arab nations.

In the 1980s and 1990s, significant improvements in computer and electronic technology ushered in unmanned aircraft systems that were far more sophisticated and maneuverable. By the late 1990s, the US Central Intelligence Agency (CIA) began deploying surveillance drones over parts of the Middle East. The CIA was active in military efforts to deploy armed drones following the September 11, 2001, terrorist attacks. The public was surprised to learn later that, in early 2002, the CIA killed three men (who turned out to be civilians) in the world's first targeted drone strike independent of an ongoing military operation. Today, drones are used regularly in targeted CIA and US military strikes from Somalia to Pakistan, and other nations in between.

CHANGING PERSPECTIVES

This history and perhaps the aggressive names of large military UAVs—the Predator and Reaper, in particular—have given drones a somewhat ominous reputation. Beyond their military uses, however, many kinds of drones have been developed over the past 15 years. Christopher Calabrese, legislative counsel to the American Civil Liberties Union (ACLU), described the ever-expanding variety of drones in a 2014 statement before the US Senate, according to an ACLU statement: "They can be

MEMBERS OF THE US MILITARY WORK ON A PREDATOR DRONE ON AN AIRFIELD IN KANDAHAR, AFGHANISTAN, IN MAY 2006. DRONES HAVE MIGRATED FROM THE BATTLEFIELD TO MANY OTHER SETTINGS IN THE LAST TWO DECADES.

for creative works. Drones are also capable of carrying more than weapons: in July 2015, the first government-approved drone delivery took place in rural southwest Virginia when a UAV dropped medical supplies into a free health clinic.

THE DRONE REVOLUTION

Thousands of hobbyists own small personal drones and fly them for leisure. In December 2015, the Teal Group aviation consulting firm estimated that about one-third of the 2 million drones sold worldwide in 2015 were purchased by US citizens. Revenue from drone sales jumped from $750 million to $1 billion between 2014 and 2015, and the number is only expected to keep growing as the popularity of private drone use grows.

That drones are becoming a regular part of American life now poses challenges for the government. How should drone use best be regulated in order to protect people from drone misuse while still allowing appropriate and beneficial UAV flight? This is an ongoing debate involving numerous government agencies and many considerations, including civil liberties, airspace and air traffic restrictions, commercial and economic concerns, and safety.

THIS DRONE, THE PARCELCOPTER, MADE FOR THE DELIVERY COMPANY DHL, IS SHOWN DURING A TRIAL RUN IN NORDDEICH, GERMANY, IN NOVEMBER 2014, TESTING ITS CAPABILITIES, INCLUDING THE ABILITY TO CARRY PARCELS.

may be used for all drones weighing 0.5 to 55 pounds (.22 to 25 kilograms). Registered drone operators are required to keep their UAVs within sight while operating them, may not fly their drones higher than 400 feet (123 meters) or near crowded public areas, and must fly at least 5 miles (8 kilometers) away from airports. This registry only addresses civilian drone users, not commercial businesses, which must apply to the FAA to receive authorization on a case-by-case basis.

The FAA hopes that assigning registration numbers and maintaining a database of drone pilots' personal information will encourage a culture of accountability among UAV enthusiasts. "Make no mistake: unmanned aircraft enthusiasts are aviators," said US transportation secretary Anthony Foxx in

BEFORE YOU FLY: B4UFLY

As of 2016, the Federal Aviation Administration's free downloadable B4UFLY app is the source of the most accurate and up-to-date flight safety information for drone hobbyists in the United States. The app's status indicator turns red in areas where flying is forbidden, and orange and yellow warnings reveal potential hazards and rules applicable to specific flight locations. The app continually updates with any changes made to FAA airspace regulations and US National Park Service regulations and easily allows private drone enthusiasts to see temporary flight restrictions in the case of natural disasters such as wildfires in the western United States.

a press release announcing the new regulations, "and with that title comes a great deal of responsibility."

However, it is not yet entirely clear how the FAA intends to enforce penalties upon private citizens who fail to register their drones or accidentally cause harm. In December 2015, the federal government set a maximum civil penalty of $27,500 on the crime of operating an unregistered UAV. It is doubtful that local law enforcement agencies chase down every passing drone to double-check its registration, but heavy fines could potentially be leveled on drone pilots who cause nuisance, injury, or damage or who trespass in no-fly zones such as around airports and government buildings.

THIS DRONE HOVERS OUTSIDE AERYON LABS, INC., IN APRIL 2016. BASED IN WATERLOO, ONTARIO, AERYON IS A PROVIDER OF ADVANCED DRONES FOR GOVERNMENT AND PRIVATE-SECTOR PURCHASERS.

ASSISTING LAW ENFORCEMENT

In 2013, according to the Associated Press, federal agents used UAVs to monitor a hostage situation in Alabama, ultimately disabling the abductor and rescuing unharmed the five-year-old child he had kidnapped. Increasingly sophisticated small drones will undoubtedly play a role in future hostage negotiations, allowing law enforcement to gain a view of captives' circumstances prior to entering a building and negotiate without the risk of a face-to-face encounter. Drones also allow a measure of increased safety in bomb investigations, offering views of the affected area before risking personnel on the ground in a potentially dangerous situation.

Drones are obviously useful when it comes to searching for missing persons, but the benefits they offer in a manhunt are not limited to basic camera functions, but also include tools like facial recognition software and license plate readers. UAVs may dramatically speed the search for individuals who are lost. This technology may also be used in the apprehension of criminals.

While commercial UAV operations are currently heavily restricted in the United States, an Ohio-based company called Persistent Surveillance Systems uses manned aircraft to monitor cities such as Juaréz, Mexico, where it captured images of 34 murders and provided evidence leading to the apprehension of the perpetrators in 2009. If the use of unmanned aerial vehicles is authorized for similar purposes, law enforcement may be able to capture evidence of crimes in progress with less expense and manpower. Dutch police have used UAVs for drug interdiction, spotting illegal marijuana grow houses with assistance from camera-equipped drones, and the technology could potentially be used to safely spot meth labs. In a less potentially ominous threat to civilian privacy, drones can also be used to take detailed recordings of crime scenes in order to preserve evidence before law enforcement professionals enter and change the scene over the course of investigation.

UAV technology. United States Customs and Border Protection (CBP) is tasked with keeping the country's borders secure, preventing acts of terrorism, and stopping illegal traffic across the country's borders.

Drones are potentially helpful tools in accomplishing these goals, and aside from the United States Defense Department, the CBP maintains the largest drone fleet within the country. A 2014 report from the *Washington Post*, however, disclosed that the CBP flew nearly 700 missions on behalf of other domestic agencies between 2010 and 2012. "Most of the missions are performed for the Coast Guard, the Drug Enforcement Administration and immigration authorities," the report stated, "but they also aid in disaster relief and in the search for marijuana crops, methamphetamine labs and missing persons, among other missions not directly related to border protection."

David V. Aguilar, former acting chief of the CBP, assured the media that requests to use the agency's UAVs were handled

A TECHNICIAN AT FORT HUACHUCA IN SIERRA VISTA, ARIZONA, CHECKS ON A PREDATOR DRONE USED BY THE AIR AND MARINE OPERATIONS (AMO) DIVISION OF CBP BEFORE ITS SURVEILLANCE FLIGHT ALONG THE US-MEXICO BORDER.

privacy. At this early stage of the drone era's legal landscape, the practice of agencies requesting assistance from CBP drones essentially gives the CBP oversight over many UAV surveillance missions conducted within the United States. According to the EFF, this practice is unacceptable without greater public transparency and appropriate privacy protections.

CHAPTER 3

DRONES DOING RESEARCH

The United States Geological Survey (USGS) first experimented with flying drones inside an active volcano when Mount St. Helens began a sustained eruption in 2004. At the time, they were found to be inferior to manned helicopters for the purpose, unable to withstand the high temperatures adequately. But a mere 10 years later, in September 2014, two men using a small off-the-shelf hobby drone and mobile GoPro camera captured detailed footage of the eruption of Iceland's Holuhraun lava field just a day before the area was completely flooded with lava.

The heat of the volcano melted the camera, but its memory card was spared, providing close-up views of a phenomenon no human could safely witness in person. In

Instead of experimenting with delivery systems, Facebook has funded the creation of a huge, solar-powered drone (reportedly as big as a Boeing 737 airplane) intended to circle Earth's stratosphere and beam wireless internet access to remote locations around the world. Called the Aquila aircraft, Facebook's pioneering Wi-Fi drone should be capable of staying aloft for three to six months, flying at heights of 60,000 to 90,000 feet (18,288–27,432 meters), far above manned airplane flights. In order to avoid the FAA's strict drone regulation, Aquila will begin testing in the United Kingdom in 2016.

Though predictions on the success of the commercial drone market vary greatly depending on the source, certain

THIS FLIGHT CHAMBER IS USED TO TEST DRONES AT AN UNMANNED AERIAL SYSTEMS MANUFACTURING FACILITY.

projections speculate that commercial UAVs in the US will become a billion-dollar industry by the 2020s. Corporate drone development in the US depends on the FAA, however, whose current restrictions make practical application of tech companies' drone programs impossible. "While it's exciting that

SIDE BY SIDE

At the time of writing, the FAA has yet to complete a comprehensive set of regulations to govern civil drone operations but instead decided whether or not to allow each instance of nongovernmental, commercial UAV flight on a case-by-case basis. Businesses that apply for special exemption may be permitted to use drone technology in "low-risk, controlled environments." A company may also be granted a Special Airworthiness Certificate (SAC) to test out new drone technology. Amazon, for example, applied for experimental airworthiness exemption in July 2014 and received an SAC for its delivery drone prototype in March 2015, by which time it was already obsolete.

The FAA ultimately granted Amazon permission to test its current-model delivery drones in the United States, provided they remain subject to the rules for individual drone hobbyists: the drones must remain below 400 feet (122 meters) in the air and 100 miles (161 kilometers) per hour in speed, remain in the pilot's line of sight at all times, and operate only in clear weather. Successful implementation of drone delivery could be a groundbreaking step for the company, but it may be some years yet before the service is up and running in the United States.